Speculative Music

Speculative Music

POEMS

Jeff Dolven

Sarabande Books
LOUISVILLE, KENTUCKY

Managing Editor
Sarabande Books, Inc.
2234 Dundee Road, Suite 200
Louisville, KY 40205

Library of Congress Cataloging-in-Publication Data

Dolven, Jeffrey Andrew.
 [Poems. Selections]
 Speculative music / Jeff Dolven.
     pages ; cm.
 ISBN 978-1-936747-58-0 (pbk. : alk. paper)
 I. Title.
 PS3604.O447S67 2013
 811'.6—dc23
                                        2013004124

Cover image by Christian Marclay.
Cover and text design by Sarabande Books.

Manufactured in Canada.
This book is printed on acid-free paper.

Sarabande Books is a nonprofit literary organization.

The Kentucky Arts Council, the state arts agency, supports Sarabande Books with state tax dollars and federal funding from the National Endowment for the Arts.

Contents

Speculative Music

How Do You Do?

All hands are out on the street today,
straining against the leashes of forearms.
Little concerned with us, they leap
to greet each other, tangle and clasp,
a subtle suction, like a kiss,
then off again in a friendly game
of overlord and underdog
we only understand in part.

Sometime later, folded in prayer,
or contemplation, right says to left,
if anything should happen to me
you'll know, won't you, what to do?
and left says to right, *you've always kept me*
friendless and illiterate.
We really ought to get them to shake,
but it's not clear that they fit that way.

Folding Star

(a star rising at folding-time;
an evening star)

My book as it lapses into the bath
  unminded, relaxes,
and now the stitches give, and the pages
  petal and fan

as though it were being eased of some pain:
  of someone's pain
it had not known of. Soon the ink,
  diluted, trickles

out with the slurry of cooling bathwater
  prattling down
through a succession of widening pipes
  to pool somewhere,

too cold now to bathe in, somewhere outside
  where the sheep are gathering
past their bedtime—pausing to drink,
  and drinking too much.

Above them an apoplectic star
  turns on itself:
once and again, quarto, octavo,
  impressively dense.

The sheep talk freely in the dark.
  The foundering shallows.
O I have taken too little care of
  care of this.

Frigidaire

I'm writing this from inside my refrigerator.
Increasingly, it's where I go when I need to think.
It turns out that the light in here is always on,
and in this shadowless space, it's easy to be good.

The obvious practical challenges are readily solved
with two or three air holes and a down jacket,
so I can focus on my main concern: that good,
being a single light reflected everywhere,

so bright and uniform you never see a shadow,
forbids you to know the many things that lie in darkness:
the insides, the behinds, of which the lying shadows
have an intimate and almost carnal knowledge.

Here, at least, I can take a proper view of the problem,
distracted only by that buzzing light, like a fly,
like a shadow you could pinch between your fingers,
pop into your mouth. It tastes like your mouth must taste.

The Whale-Road

For DGB

I set out early on the whale-road,
and it was a fine day for it.
   The way was clear, and my hands were sweet
with ambergris.

I could tell he'd passed not long before:
a river of strong salt air
   buoyant like an epsom bath
trails in his wake.

It lifts my spirits! I have high hopes
I'll catch him yet on the whale-road,
   for though he's strong, he labors somewhat
up the hills

on account, I'm sure, of his carnival girth
and his hurdy-gurdy breathing,
   those Sunday lungs, most musical,
most melancholy.

Sometimes, I'm told, he'll pitch himself
like a kind of roadside church:
   a faithful assistant mounts his back
tall as a steeple

and proceeds to draw, one then another,
countless silken scarves
   of barrel-organ crimson from
his spiracle.

I do my best to catch the tune
on my harmonica,
   my silver mouth-harp, sharp to taste
as a hook in the mouth.

This is a City of Bridges

This is a city of bridges,
though the water is mostly fled;
a city of ambitious span
and empty bed.

It makes for a curious skyline:
from the road you'd think
of skyscrapers at a watering hole
stooping to drink

except that there's no water.
The old canals are parched,
and no one comes to sing or suckle
under an arch

and no one quite remembers
what the bridges were for,
what we were getting over, and why
we're still building more.

But build we do. More bridges!
Bridges to make us free.
At the foot of each the traveler has
a choice of three

but nowhere to rest at nightfall
when the bridges chase their tails,
churning between dusk and dawn
like buried wheels.

A Brief Life of Hermogenes

in pueritia senex: in senectute infans

He was born in Tarsus, a gifted child:
they say that his first word was "first."
From the beginning, everything followed,
each word linked to the next as though
in some metaphysical cursive, his hand
never needing to leave the page.
(Not his literal hand, of course: it was talk,
but it made everyone think of writing.)

In his short pants he stood in the pasture
calling the animals names, haranguing
the sheep and the goats that crowded round
as his gorgeous epithets fell in loops
about their necks. The farmhands marveled,
how the beasts deferred to him:
scuffing their hooves, tipping their heads,
newly ashamed of their rude voices.

He spoke in the city before his first beard,
a prodigy, drawing prodigious crowds,
though even then his intimates
sensed the faltering of his gift.
He wrote some books of rhetoric,
but as a man his talk became
at length a kind of musical babble,
sung to himself, or to a god.

So when he died, they cut him open,
and there was foaled from his speechless chest—
the histories agree on this—

9

there was whelped from his dumbstruck chest
a heart blood-slick with fine, black hair.
It must have looked like a baby's head.
When word got round, for days it was all
that anyone could talk about.

Morning Czar and Evening Tsar

Up on the highest balcony,
the *coup d'etat du jour*:
   the Morning Czar has fallen.
Long live the Evening Tsar!

There's dancing in the central square
as the snow begins to fall;
   we'll know our friends by their dueling scars
   and the Fabergé glitter in their eyes:
the mood is festival.

Now, someone says he's seen him—
the Evening Tsar, I mean—
   and his beard is black as they say, he says,
   and his cheeks as red, and never mind
   the rumors about the family,
how easily they bleed

one into the other,
and the other into one:
   for the *philosophes* have gone to bed
   and the dancing masters have their way
   and the snow hangs weightless in the air
   and this time, finally, spells the end,
till all the spelling's done.

One wonders what's become of him.
The Morning Czar, I mean.
   Meantime, we turn each other round
   like gemstones cut to hold a light

that never rises, never sets
and flatters dance and dancer both,
and we'll never again be caught at dawn
in our evening clothes, again.

Cantaloupe

If, after so many blunders, we pick the lock
of the cantaloupe, it will keep its promise to sing,
trilling the tongue long coiled in its gut like a snake:

the tongue no botanist has ever wrung
from its seedy heart, nor gourmet ever found
limp on his plate when the summer meal was done.

So hold the brave new fruit with both your hands
and feel its tumblers turn; or better still,
between your fingers take the dangling end

of the coarse twine that's knotted round its hull,
and follow it—like a melody you've sung
before, but backward—till the song unspools

and leaves the naked melon's single lung
heaving with rare delight. Now listen closely,
and don't flinch if, at last, you feel its tongue—

muscular, quivering—thrust impetuously
into your ear. Think hard before you answer
its impossible overture: *marry me, marry me*.

You've Been Dry

You've been dry, so you've been drinking,
and now it's late and nothing's done.
It's going to go hard with yourself
tomorrow, if you can't make good.

So harness the team, and hitch the plough,
but you're still drunk, and the stars are fluting
around the sky like the birds at dawn—
too many melodies to follow.

The next morning, it's hard to bear
the mess you've made of the neighbor's field,
though the sun can see the crazy furrows
carve out a map of your cracked hand.

Faith and Hope

When I was young my parents left me
every day, and I was raised
by chairs—wild child in a serious tribe.

They spent a lot of time at prayer
was what I used to think. As plain
as day the table in their midst.

I despaired of such piety, but if
they saw into my doubting heart
they never folded up their laps

or punished me for having dreams
where they lay toppled on the kitchen floor,
thrashing their legs like panicked beetles.

Now, when your chair scrapes the floor
I always wince. I need a new law.
Make me put my head in your lap.

Rituals

Washing your hands, trying the lock,
.burning a hundred head of cattle
not to eat, washing your hands
again, trying the lock again,
talking forever to yourself,
saying the sorts of things the god
most can't understand, who finally
figures *this must be for me*.

Horse Lessons

Lesson 1

First, the zipper, right in the middle:
a round-trip number wound in a circle,
girth of us both, with teeth to suture
frontlegs to hindlegs, fore to aft.
Your part, you put it on like your pants,
then pull the pants up over your head
(think ragtop on a rainy day):
the zipper should be dangling there
right about between your legs.

Ahem: now clear your mind, and grasp
the tag with your right hand, tongue with your left,
insert the tongue, etcetera,
then swing your right hand over your head,
making an O—O for *omega*,
O for *omphalos*—counterclockwise
till you've zipped yourself in the dark,
dark as the day before you were born
and what have you got yourself into now
but nothing more than the whole horse.

Lesson 2

So what is this sense of gratitude?
—as though for some surprising reunion,
some last-second suture, or suitable match?
You're right to ask. There was a time

17

when none of us was alone in his skin,
nobody nothing but a mind in hide.
Days of clover! before the knacker,
the tanner, the cleaver, the handy man,
and the sad confusion of the aftermath,
with everyone looking for his other half.
The aft his head. The head his aft.

Lesson 3

A list of habits to unlearn:
bipedalism, table manners,
counting, whistling, washing, catch.
Harder, being braced to catch,
then proud to hold, then having, too,
for richer, poorer, sickness, health,
you name it, time to let it go,
you name it, then, in time, you won't,
and then you'll have one habit left.
That's right, the suit.

                It's dark inside,
and warm, and close, a little tight,
but this is true of everybody,
is it not? And so?

           It's like
you're hungry and you don't yet know
just what it is you're hungry for,

or whom, exactly, you should ask.
The suit will tell you what to do.

Lesson 4

But perhaps we're getting ahead of ourselves.
Some background, then! You may recall
the ancient Greeks, in a time of trouble,
who built themselves a horse for riding
inside-out.

       The men inside
were bound by friendship, family,
and shared experience of war,
bound to be at each other's throats
except that day for the horse they shared,
that wooden horse with the single trick,
the stoical trick of standing still.

That day they sat on their hands all day—
no clasping, no shaking, no fists or gifts—
sat on their hands and stood on all fours,
and that with a certain equipoise.

Lesson 5

Now, how to walk. Not how a table
ambles, legs straight, back stable.

More like falling into step,
equable, companionable,
and single file. No saddle.

Lesson 6

Horse walks into a bar. He says
nothing. Since when can horses talk?
(At least not before he's had a drink,
a stiff drink, or somebody has.)

Horse walks into a bar. Somebody
hands him a drink. Another trick:
plenty of handsome riders here,
waiting for him to overreach.

Horse walks into a bar. Walks in,
a nifty bit of horsemanship.
Not that he's here for kicks, mind you.
Not that he's here to kick back.

Horse walks into a bar. "Hey buddy,
why the long face?" He's heard that before.
Remember, a horse is nobody's buddy.
He's nobody's buddy and he doesn't mind.

Lesson 7

Next, the trot. You put one foot
in front of the other, or maybe better,
askance—athwart—you left, that is,
I right, you right, I left, and then
only the horse is left. Am I right?

Lesson 8

What to do with an itch, you'd think,
depends on the itch. The itch *ab extra*
merits a switch or a swift kick.
The itch *ab intra* is harder to reach,
stretching around outside yourself
to get back in: aye, there's the rub.
The catch.

        But really which is which
is a difference that shouldn't come
between us. After all, an itch
is something you catch from somebody else
again: ergo, it touches us not;
ergo, the moral is: don't scratch.

Lesson 9

Canter: that's former, then midmost, then hinder,
traveling faster and not without pleasure,
the rhythm of so much mortal conjecture
and harmless enough, if you're sure to remember
not to seek rest in any such measure.

Lesson 10

Do you remember the short chute,
the ambivalent grip, the heave and the hands
waiting to catch you, waiting to hand you
the deed, the keys, the change, the reins?
You don't? Then may I recommend
a sudden tumble onto the grass,
up before you know you're up,
pitching yourself on the pitching deck
of a spring wind swept green field.

What it feels like being born
is something every beast of burden
wants to know, whatever the burden.
I want you to remind me—no,
I want to remember. Failing that,
I'll settle for being mixed together
in the final organ grinder,
door to the dog-eat-horse hereafter.
Squeeze right through like we belong there.

Lesson 11

Meantime, beware: when darkness falls
you may hear singing from the other
side of the suit. The skin. Let's say
it sounds like someone you used to know.
Don't answer her, especially if
she calls you names, familiar names,
and don't flinch if you feel her hands,
familiar hands, so cool and soft,
glide across this bristling belly
as though they could smooth the hair away.
Her fingers are feeling for the seam.

> *What is twice as silent*
> *and ridden from inside,*
> *unfathomably obvious*
> *and rapt in hide?*

Remember the Greeks in their horse-shaped box,
that stoical box, surrounded by doubts:
they're in that box like a racing gate,
waiting for the end to begin.

> *What's emptiest of husbands*
> *and riddled without sons?*
> *Does none of them hear my lovely voices,*
> *Lovely ones?*

> *What goes on all fours mornings,*

and noons and evenings too?
Come out, come out, come out, come out
and say we do.

What can we do? Remember this:
a man sleeps lying down in his bed,
a man sleeps slack, and lays down his weight,
and he frets when he has to sleep alone.
His body's alone and his mind reels.
Better to sleep on four braced feet,
and neither lie, nor lean, nor dream.

Lesson 12

What happens at a gallop is
the mystery. A-one-step, two-step,
three-step, four-step, somewhere there
we're all suspended, up off the ground,
hoist by one another's bootstraps.

Lesson 13

My part, I put it on like a shirt—
a hair-shirt, neckless, hemmed with steel,
the bright brocade of the zipper's teeth—
but the inside's lined with felt so soft
I scarcely feel it, just the subtlest
pinch at the temples, like a crown.

I look out through the big glass eyes
and everything is clear and distinct.
Behind my I eyes I feel your patience.

I do, I confess—absurd, I know—
I sometimes want to turn around
to face—you feel for me, I know,
but what? I can hardly bear to think.

And still I feel we have some kind
of understanding—here in the gate,
at pasture, under siege, on terms
of strictest equanimity,
and standing up, together, fast,
standing fast, ready for nothing,
this is what the horse stands for.

My Puppets

I wake up mornings snug in my bed-puppet.
Not the liveliest in my repertoire,
but wait, it gets better: next is my pants-puppet,
bandy-legged, hyperactive, true
to life, puppeting life-like down the hall
onto the waiting elevator car

(my marionette) then down, down to my bus-
puppet, puppeting all those nodding heads,
those drowsy fingers on their so-called smart phones,
and wait till you get to see my office-puppet,
a *tour de force* of digitalization
that makes the market flap its arms in panic.

So this must be my poem-puppet, yes?
Don't be naïve. The poem is my hand.
Can't you feel it here inside you, friend?
It enters where it can, and reaches up,
way up behind your eyes. So realistic,
how your mouth moves like that as you read.

Peach Bone

There's a pearl of marrow in the middle of the peach bone,
the sweetest part of the peach—the only part
you want, in fact, whether you know it or not.

Come on, you really thought a peach was a fruit?
It's just as American as you or me,
marbled with fat, like everybody here,

you bet your eyeteeth, ladies and gentlemen,
gentlemen, ladies—that choice, I leave to you—
come on, admit it, whatever you want is meat.

The Labor Theory of Value

Coachman, carry me home tonight!
Horsemen, keep a stately pace!
Highwaymen, make way, make way—
lie on your bellies, we go on your backs.

When I arrive, let the doorman turn
smartly on his smooth left heel;
the houseboys shall stand in ranks around,
facing outward, shoulders squared.

When the chairman stoops to bear my weight,
I'll know I've got where I belong,
though nothing quite keeps out the draft—
so cold I scarcely feel my wealth.

So fireman, fireman! Dance for me!
Let your fingertips crackle like castanets!
—But I fear he will not want to dance
alone. No sleep for me tonight.

Shame School

A new semester starts today at Shame School.
Semester: what a mortifying word,
like *seminar*, or worse still, *semiotics*.
"Say *semiotics!*" says the photo man,
and laughs at us as he opens his shutter wide.

Now, I don't mean the school next to St. Peter's:
the nuns there teach the boys to dress in layers,
even, or especially, in dreams.
They sit and sweat through—dreadful word—
assembly, whitewash running down their faces.

And not the school down by the river, either:
they go to classes with their flies unzipped
for fear of whipping. You know them anywhere,
dissembling—ugh—on corners, blurting out
their rote confessions of unseemly acts.

No: Shame School is all rigorous technique:
the seven shades of blush, played as a scale
from cool to hot and back again, and again,
and again; the dip and wheel of a rigorous cringe,
like shot-put, but without the sweet release.

Here, photo day is just another test.
"*Semantics!*" It takes multiple exposures
before you really seem what you mean to seem.
Success at Shame School is an open secret:
practice, practice, until you're like to die.

The Force of Precedent

Suppose I knock a good man down,
knock him down *per accidens*,
walking the orchard boundary
here on my ancestral grounds.

Suppose I could prove I've taken that walk,
that very walk, each day for years,
just as my father did before:
honoris causa, down the man goes.

Consider please a ruddy fruit,
a ready fruit, on a low branch,
spoiling for it, *felix culpa*,
headed south, *pro bono*—

boom! He's *a posteriori*.
I rest my case, and best of all,
the man allows the blame is his,
as he has been knocked down before.

Quarter

Catch! It's a quarter, right? You got it? Good.
Now, pinch the flat between your first two fingers,
press hard against the milling with your thumb,
and *pop!* it's inside out, unbuttoned and plump,
like a lychee fruit or a raw scallop.

Can't just put it back in your pocket, can you?
A coin shouldn't care whether it's heads or tails,
whether it's warm on your thigh, or cold in a drawer,
but what you've got there is strangely sensitive.
It twitches in your palm—or is that you?

It isn't you, but you can tell it wants
something. Soothing, maybe. Hard to be sure.
It's like a ganglion, a knot of nerves,
but whose? It's like a pain, but fortunately
a pain that's being felt by someone else.

How the Fire Feels

The other night, you kicked the dog:
the dog was making too much noise
so you kicked him hard, and he barked back, loud.
You thought you knew what you were doing
but your brother said

> *think how the dog feels*

and he left the room with tears in his eyes,
and you kicked yourself, you should have known,
but it probably didn't hurt enough
and the dog got back to barking again
and your sister said

> *think how your brother feels*

and the heating coil curls like a snake
on a rock in the sun on top of the stove,
and it hisses at you in a transport of fear
when you reach out to touch it, just for kicks,
and your father says

> *think how the fire feels.*

Alcibiades' Waltz

If Socrates is a man
and all men are mortal
then Socrates is mortal.

If Socrates is thirsty
after a long day talking,
then Socrates is a man,

right? and deserves a drink.
And if the night wears on
and the talk turns to love

and the wine sings from the cup
then Socrates is mortal,
surely. And if—and if—

and if the musicians are playing,
softly, for themselves,
and the wine sleeps on the floor—

asking a woman to dance,
asking a man to dance,
one, two, three.

May I have the next dance?
Socrates is a man.
All men are merely mortal.

The Dressing Room

You fall asleep in a room in a house that was made for you,
all dressed up and asleep in a bed you didn't make,
asleep in your shirt, in your size, your sleeve and neck and chest.

You wake undressed in another room, a dressing room.
You barely notice the walls are bare. The fatherly clerk
greets you sitting down, his arms aswoon with coats.

He's dressed in evening clothes bespeaking another era,
melancholy black, long tails between his legs.
He passes the garments one by one. They are unclean.

Sweat and blood and want have worked into the weave.
The stains fall naturally over your scars and your hungriest parts.
He winces at the fit each time, until his arms

are empty and his sleepless eyes confess he's down
to one last hope: *is this a dream?* Of course it is,
you say. For here you are to blame for everything.

Strawberries and Cream

[As a proof of the impossibility of artificial intelligence] the inability
to enjoy strawberries and cream may have struck the reader as
frivolous. Possibly a machine might be made to enjoy this delicious
dish, but any attempt to make one do so would be idiotic.
                    (Alan Turing, "Computing Machinery and Intelligence")

It doesn't make the *mmmmmm* you might expect
(the level drone refrigerators dream
in nights of never tasting what's inside),
rather bumps along, its irregular rhythms
expressing subtleties of pleasure I,
its sole creator, cannot always discern.
But what a comfort when it's working well:
somewhere in its heart a filament thrills
with unreflective pleasure, like a child's.

It savors this fruit it never had to choose;
it does not bore or sicken, grow out or up
or old. It runs a tireless electric tongue
over the skin, the dimples plugged with seeds
like mattress buttons, the wrinkled sheets of cream.
Nothing is diminished or consumed;
the feeling is so pure it can be hard
to tell the thing's turned on at all. Sometimes
I lie for hours, listening to be sure.

After Work

After work I went to the Post Office
having been preoccupied
all day with the daily prospect of
an urgent parallelogram

from a friend from whom I had endured
many degrees of separation.
Someone had to be the first
to set things right—this couldn't last—

but the postman wept when I arrived.
"Just give it to me straight," I said.
"I can't," he sobbed. "It's gotten bent
and spindled, folded, mutilated."

So it had, an angry ball
of unapologetic angles;
my disappointment was acute
enough to cut your finger on

when all at once I recognized
this origami masterwork
was fold for fold the crumpled note
I would have penned and thrown away

tomorrow. Who knows better, friend,
than the squares of the U.S. Postal Service
how it's never too late for love
to take whatever shape it takes.

Relax, Relax

How long do you have to be awake
before you can't go back to sleep?
Before you have to call it a night,
rub your eyes, and start again.

Unless it's always back to sleep,
like the planets slipping into reverse,
lapsing back across the sky:
epicycles, they used to say,

loops like the loops of a telephone cord,
which ran (remember?) hand-to-wall
but had so many second thoughts,
turning back on itself again

like the sleeper, curled around some thing
that happened only yesterday,
but never only yesterday.
And was it only yesterday

I was riding away, on my epicycle?
Further, further, wondering how far
the cord would stretch, and straighten, till
a sudden jerk: and now, I'm back.

Sometimes I Smile

Turn on the light: I have to tell you something.
Sometimes I smile before I mean it. Better,
sometimes I've smiled before I mean it. Meant it.
You know what I mean?—Sometimes I smile before
I smile, or know I'm smiling, and I mean it,
although I didn't mean to—never mind—

or maybe, sometimes in the street I rise
my arm, I *raise* my arm, before I know
who's there, or who you are, before I've raised
the question, why, I've waved, or better, waved
away whatever doubts or hopes or doubts
arose, and well before I had a reason,

waking you—I don't know what I want
until I wanted to, or you, and you,
I must have known you long before I knew
you wanted, too, but how will you have known
except already, look, our lampshade, it's a rose,
and look, the light's out. Quick, put out the light!

The Invention: A Libretto for Speculative Music

Dramatis Personae: Inventor

Invention

Reporter

Spouse

Six Musicians

Blindness. Darkness, rather: for now there is a single red light, glowing like an on-switch, or the tip of a cigarette. It hovers, indolently, center stage. Behind, as one's eyes adjust, six mute forms, a seventh moving among them, and—click—*now two are visible stage right, the* INVENTOR *and a* MUSICIAN, *lit by the lamp on the* MUSICIAN'S *music stand; the* INVENTOR *turns on the lamp, and as he does so, the* MUSICIAN *begins to play. The* INVENTOR *passes out of the first pool of light and*—click—*into another, bringing the next* MUSICIAN *to life, and then the next. The music, accumulating part by part, is angular and self-impeding. The instruments encounter each other like hurried travelers in the great hall of a railway station: moving in opposite directions, they meet, stop short, dodge left, then right, then again, a ballet of perfect courtesy and perfect obstruction. Rather like trying, on a busy morning, to slip past oneself in the mirror and carry on. But, no.*

Now the six lamps on the MUSICIANS' *six stands are lit, forming a semicircle, and bringing to light in turn a box the size and shape of an upright piano, with its back to the audience. On top, the* INVENTION *reclines in the attitude of a cabaret chanteuse, smoking, otherwise still. Its face is cast in darkness. Blindness, rather. The* INVENTOR *keeps his distance as he moves among the* MUSICIANS, *alternately attentive and distracted. He pauses in his irregular rounds, turns, pauses again, starts to sing:*

INV.   I have an idea: strip out the frets.

No rungs or steps. No lets. No ratchets.

Unplug the valves. Grease up the slide.

Don't punctuate. Elide. Elide.

—What was I saying? Damn violins!

The bow runs out. You count your sins.
The oboe fails at the end of the breath.
Between the last and the next one—now,
where was I?—Should be getting home.
I think I hear the metronome.

He takes a violin abruptly from one of the MUSICIANS, *sights down the fingerboard, turns it upside down, shakes it, holds it at arm's length as something suddenly, utterly strange, then hands it gently back.*

INV.   I have an idea: string a string,
        steel, or gut, through everything.
        String a string—now to then—
        or am I repeating myself again?

He hesitates once more. The pause is rather long, and though the music is chattering on, its cross-purposes do not do much to make the interval pass more quickly. I do hope you are finding this interesting. At last, behind him, the REPORTER *enters, scribbling deliberately on a stenographer's pad. He sings, and writes down his song as he sings it, or perhaps sings it off the page as he writes it, in a rhythmless, documentary plainchant. He does not look up as he walks downstage.*

REP.   —an unconfirmed rumor has it—
        an unnamed source—a little bird—
        as someone—wind of which—was heard—
        alleged invention—said to make—
        purportedly—the eyeteeth ache—
        the blood to turn—harmonically—
        back in its round—arresting sound—
        alleged inventor—mere hearsay—
        impossible, say some—to play—
        nonsense—it plays itself—some say—

By now he is standing next to the INVENTOR. *Both men rock uneasily on their feet, out of time with one another, and with the music, which is still obdurately out of time with itself.*

INV.   You're here to ask about my loote?
        Coins ring changes down a chute.

As the INVENTOR *sings, the* REPORTER *transcribes each word a beat behind, and sings it off his page in that flat, one-off echo. He is shaking his head as he writes.*

INV.   Or my hapsichord? Old-fashioned sound.
        The keys change places when you turn around.
        Famous for that one. Some time ago.
        Forget the score. You're good to go.
        My guitarrh: you catch it by the throat—
        but it's getting late. You have your coat?
        Tick tick tick. So nice to talk.
        And tick again. Should fix that clock.

REP.   —check—but is it—double check—
        our sources—off the record—say—
        their sources say—there's something new—

INV.   Where are you from? The *Mirror*? The *Star*?
        No news here. Sorry you came so far.
        Nothing happened. Don't know how.
        What's the use remembering now?

REP.   —nothing—happened—reportedly
        he said—supposedly—said he—

All this time the INVENTION *is idling at the center of the stage, unmoving save for an occasional puff of smoke; it is indifferent to the exchange, bored or simply elsewhere, in a manner that may call to mind an old acquaintance, perhaps one in particular, then again perhaps not, at the surrendering end of certain squandered evenings. As the* REPORTER *draws nearer, however, something in the* INVENTION'S *languor tenses. The tip of its cigarette is brighter, perhaps? And when he stands next to it, it begins, without looking at him, or anyone, to murmur in sympathy.*

41

REP.   —pending further—fit to print—
         —review—revive—river of ink—

He steps backward in surprise, looking up from his pad for the first time: the
INVENTION'S voice, a lush, insinuating rasp, has slipped in with his, following
his unhandsome monody, or perhaps keeping it company. Or, for a moment, leading?
He looks into its face. It does not look back. He steps forward again and continues to
sing, and his pen scratches to a halt, and his voice comes free of it.

REP.   —a river of ink—beginning where—
         so clear—great height—and pure, up there,
         and rare, bright ichor trickling down
         through leaves and grass, between the stones,
         picking up grit, hits the streets,
         back streets, back rooms, cul de sacs,
         darkening, thickening, gathering facts
         and now it's black and fit to print,
         impressed on sheets, hot off the stands,
         rubbing off on our fingers' ends,
         onto our lips—unmistakable,
         the taste, ash, acid, hint of apple.

Now the REPORTER'S notebook has fallen unregarded to the floor, and he stands
beside the INVENTION in an attitude of startled rapture: its voice has joined his
altogether, first in unison, then in harmony, moving now with, now companionably
against the descending phrases by which they are finding the way out of his
narrow range. Moments like this, perhaps, are what was wanted—but now, the
REPORTER, he rests his hand on the piano-box and closes his eyes.

REP.   Every page finds its end
         is flames: quick tinder in the ear
         or burning slowly underground,
         ink will out, will rise as smoke,
         an incense in the lungs, as soot
         that blacks the blood and makes a blot
         of knowledge in the certain mind.

Impetuously he pulls the INVENTION'S *hand to his lips, and takes a deep drag from its cigarette. The mutual estrangement of the* MUSICIANS *has been repaired; what was once a self-confounding crowd is now more like a flock of starlings, who fill the air with figures of spontaneous collaboration, a great airshow in the high gallery of the railway station—you recall, my figure of the railway station?—which is now a concert hall, and now the open sky; the morning mirror, blocked once by the obstructing self, now somehow shows the way. The duet between* REPORTER *and* INVENTION *is echoed in these figures, or anticipated, as the music explores its singers with increasing confidence and curiosity.*

REP.   As though the echo called the tune,
        as though the ink could draw the pen,
        the ink that inks the *Daily Mirror*:
        remember mirror now remember.

As they sing, the INVENTOR *stands off to the side. It is impossible to say if he is listening. Time is passing, as I hardly need to tell you, quite some time, and not unpleasantly, in fact I would not wish it less, though one can see that the* REPORTER'S *hand, resting lightly on the piano-box, is now bearing more of his weight; and his voice begins to weaken, though perhaps you will agree, even its skips and halts are ornaments of great beauty and pathos. He is singing on his knees now. Marvelous, no? Now he lapses finally to the floor, a slow diminuendo, until he is lying motionless and silent. Ash from the cigarette drops on his jacket. The* INVENTION *is unmoved and unmoving. And now, oh dear: as you can hear, the music disintegrates again, though the original confusion has become something more like the endgame of an overlong dinner party, each* MUSICIAN *falling into periodic, weary silence—sometimes all silent together, long enough that you wonder if it will ever start again. It does, each time—now—and again—each time so far, with fragments of new effort standing sporadic vigil over the* REPORTER'S *still form. Now, I must assume, you are starting to wonder, how long will this latest interlude, this indefinite intermittence, go on? As am I, I assure you—but now a woman enters from the wings, tangling and untangling her hands. She sings in a continuous stream, with occasional gasps for breath, and the* MUSICIANS *rally in new agitation around her.*

SP.   —singing along, singing along,
        when a heel slips on the topmost stair,

singing along, the song that stitches
morning to midday, midday to after-
noon, when the tire loses its grip
on the ice, singing along, when the plane
fails to arrive, and the song skips,
and the tune—the tune—the tune—the after-
noon is waiting for the night,
singing alone, didn't come home,
something is wrong, singing along—

*She is crossing the stage from left to right—singing along, singing along—and
now she sees the* REPORTER *lying beside the* INVENTION. *She starts, stops,
and she is down on her knees by his side, a handsome woman, all the melodrama
notwithstanding, and there is something impressively fierce about how she turns him
on his back—really, such a show of force—but still, do you not think, impressively
fierce, how she turns him on his back and loosens his collar,* singing along,

SP.   —singing along, something was wrong,
           didn't come home, singing alone,
           how long—so long—before the song—

As she sings and ministers, the INVENTION, *so still, begins to take an interest,
expressed again in a subtle quickening of its easy repose, the brighter glowing of that
cigarette.*

SP.   —but wait, a beat—and just in time!—
           a-one, a-two—a beat—how song—
           a-one, a-two, safe down the stairs,
           a-three, to rest on the side of the road,
           and the plane, a-four, it touches down,
           right on time, with that sweet smoke
           of wheels on tarmac, skid and kiss
           touching down on the tip of the tongue
           just as the perfect word arrives,
           just in time, just as the note

44

skips down the stairs from the circling spheres
nine at a time to light on the tip
of the violin bow, just in time
to play its part, prodding the heart
on to the next beat—next after that—

Like the REPORTER, *the* SPOUSE *has been joined as she sings by the* INVENTION, *in a duet that first astonishes, then transports her—listen now, you can hear—*

SP.   —and everywhere now, airplanes are landing,
bringing the word from far away places,
everyone making all their connections,
everyone safe, coming safe home,
even who've never been home before—
a-one, a-two, a-three, a-four—

As she sings, she rises to her feet, and leans into the song; at the height of her reverie, she turns to the INVENTION *and kisses it, deeply, on the mouth. A moment, please; a moment. The music surges. Smoke drifts upward when their lips part. The crescendo seems to rouse the* REPORTER, *who looks up to see them in this embrace. Startled, he moves backward, away from the* INVENTION; *now, you hear how their songs overlap, hers in harmony with the* INVENTION, *his alone and at odds:*

SP.   —a-five, a-six, a-seven, eight,
we'll never be lost, we'll never be late—

REP.   —my eyes—I don't—such doubts about
—believe—my doubts about—my eyes—

Now the REPORTER *stumbles to his feet as she sings, and moves toward her, taking her hands in his, to plead, or to pull her away; she resists, and raises her arms— perhaps this is a moment for an intermission? forgive me, it is all happening rather quickly—but ah, now, a hand has fallen to his back, settling there, another falls to her waist, and now—marvelous!—they are by some unpremeditated consent, or so it appears, and however awkwardly, dancing together.*

SP.   and any fear—
       why who—oh dear—
       or have we met—

The dance quickly becomes, how shall I say, practiced? accomplished? and then something rather better than that. It is smart sort of two-step, I remember it from before the last war, or was it before the war before that, but perhaps you are too young? I do not doubt—I hope it is not forward to say so—that you would quickly get a feel for it. And as they dance, they start to sing together, in unison and now in harmony, three voices now.

S. & R.   how—intricate—
           it seems we know
           this one, the next
           step and the next
           a-one, a-two,
           it's like a text
           we've memorized
           except who can
           remember when?

Is this perhaps a moment to ask, or would it be a distraction: has this ever happened to you, could you imagine, with a lover, or with the fruit vendor, or with the people at the train station, on the airplane, suddenly discovering that you both, or you all, know the words to a song you have never heard before? And you start to sing it together. Had you ever, is it too much to ask, understood anyone before? Does it not seem sad, the taking turns of ordinary talk, all the different words parceled out, your words and mine? Perhaps this has never happened to you. Perhaps this has never happened; and of course, of course, I know, it is not exactly happening now? A-one, a-two— their dance grows in confidence and verve, faltering only, a stutter, an incipient stumble, when their momentum carries them away from the INVENTION, and so they learn, I would say instinctively, would you not?—to stay close, describing narrow and elegant circles while it sings and smokes in the center.

S. & R.   Who leads, who follows,
           who can say

mirror mirror
both of us
coming and going
both at once
each word, each step
coming to mind
and body both
and going, gone,
the same new song
the same next breath
to be in love
or out of love
is nothing to
the bliss of this
unwritten script
already read
whoever sang
whoever danced
except who can
remember now?

The whirl is so giddy, and so effortless, that they do not notice the INVENTOR
*is approaching from the back of the stage until, at that last word, "now," he takes
the cigarette from the* INVENTION'S *hand and briskly stubs it out on the piano-
box. At once—no, not quite at once, but now, as you hear, it is done—the dancing
and the singing stop, and the* MUSICIANS *fall out again with one another. The*
REPORTER *and* SPOUSE *stand in confusion. They sing, simultaneously but not
together, as the* INVENTOR *begins distractedly to shepherd them toward the back
of the stage.*

REP.   —hearsay—see here—what sources say—
         what happened—what authority—

SP.   —where are we going? the song—it's stopped—
         be careful now—the broken step—

They look back at the INVENTION, *which is once more idle and indifferent. The* INVENTOR *is still urging them along.*

INV.   Got to be careful. Might blow a fuse.

Lousy way to make the news.

You say you're from the *Daily Planet*?

Give 'em my best. Ought to visit.

I have an idea: come round tomorrow.

I'll show you my mechanical sparrow.

Tail's the bellows, beak's a whistle.

Sings all day. You got your pencil?

Your pad? So sorry you have to run.

Forgetting anything? Do write soon!

He ushers them out; they leave slowly, wordlessly, with unsteady steps. It is among the most touching scenes of the evening, and I wish you could see the not quite clasping of their hands as they leave the stage. But now—ah, now: the "now," I fear, that means "next"—but now the INVENTOR *begins his rounds again in reverse, circling the back of the stage, stopping by each* MUSICIAN'S *stand and—click—turning out the light. A-four, a-three, a-two, a-one. The stage grows darker and darker, and the music, by subtraction, sparer and sparer. He sings to himself as he goes:*

INV.   I have an idea: string a string,

steel, or gut, through everything.

String a string through everyone.

Or am I repeating myself again?

A-none: the last light clicks off; the last MUSICIAN *falls silent. Darkness? Blindness? Is this the end? Your coat—but wait, now there is the kiss and flare of a struck match, as the* INVENTOR *lights the* INVENTION'S *cigarette again, and they are together in the small circle of its roseate glow. They start to sing.*

INV.   We have been singing together nights

for how long now? This dry white throat

wells up with ink and in the heat

the ink turns smoke and blacks the black

between the stars. They're written there,
the words to all the songs we know.
The sky's night is a palimpsest—

He steps away, and turns back to face the INVENTION; *he is at the periphery of
its red light, and his voice is disentangled.*

INV.   —but I don't remember anything
            myself. I'm old. I lose the tune.
            The feeling is so altogether
            new each time. Each time so—now,
            now, where was I? Now, who are you?

Throughout the INVENTOR'S *halting recitative, the* INVENTION *has been
looking evenly into the darkness, looking toward where we sit, if it is looking at all.
Now it takes a last drag, breathes the smoke out into the empty air, and stubs out the
cigarette for itself. Darkness again.*

*We are waiting together in that darkness, now, and silence, you and I. How long
have we been here? What is going to happen next? Do you know this story, after all?
Perhaps the evening is truly over. Patience—I am reminding myself; I am sometimes
hasty in taking leave, or I have been, in the past. There is a decorous interval that
ought to elapse before getting up from one's seat, before I take your arm and guide
you down the row, up the aisle, out into the lobby, where we can all see one another
again in the bright mirrors—forgive me, not all of us, but you understand—mirrors
that may guide us, in the lingering society of what we have seen together, out under
the night sky. I do hope you are pleased that I brought you here. Or dare I hope, that
you brought me? I wonder, either way, if the present interval is long enough to ask
you—may I?—what you thought of it all. I do like to think I have some idea.*

Splinter

I am singing now of the splinter of wood
you got in your knee as a child and never
got out. Of the splinter that sank out of sight
in your flesh and was gone.

I am singing of something that cannot be lost,
that cannot be changed like your clothes or your voice
(your voice that sinks over time to a low
and incredulous moan

as you know); I am singing of something that cannot
be found, as the querying steel first confessed
in her gentle now outlasted ministering hand
who sought it in vain;

I am singing of something loose in your blood
where it roves without homecoming, never turns back,
traveling even when you are at rest:
that wears you away

like the diamond tip of a phonograph needle
tracking the seams of your bones, scoring
the delicate tissues, and singing *I
am the splinter of wood;*

I am singing the truth that your skin tries to hide:
that within you are only the wound that you got
as a child on your knees on the splintering floor,
or sometime before.

Hummingbird

If you keep your head still long enough,
and level, a humming bird will come
and stand in the air next to your ear:

and the bird will dip his beak in the dark,
working in patient, meticulous circles,
until your ear is perfectly clean.

The humming of a hummingbird
is because it doesn't know the words,
and neither, it would seem, do you,

though now his offices arc done
all sounds are newborn clear and keen
and singular as different species.

Here's the Thing

So I'm putting the needle down on the record,
and here's the thing—or I'm turning the dial
till the static dies, or picking up
the phone, hello?—and here's the thing—

the music hasn't started yet,
and nobody's started talking, either,
and here's the thing—there's still a there
there in the crackling silence. Hear?

It's like you've entered another room
without leaving the room you're in,
and now you're under the maestro's sway
who's holding everybody's breath.

Or it's like you hear for yourself at last
the planets spinning in their grooves,
the radio hiss of their gentle rounds,
infinite space in a telephone booth

and here's the thing, the telephone.
You say you're coming? Hear, hear!
You say you're leaving? There, there.
I still can't hear you—damn this thing—

Hello? Hello? Am I still there?

Humilitas

You've got a big body, bumble bee,
a big body and such little wings!
And blimey, such a cumbersome name,
"bumble," like "stumble" or "grumble." Crumbs!

You don't flutter so much as you fumble,
dog-paddle from petal to petal,
hind-legs clotted with pollen enough
to fill, if you're lucky, a wee tumbler,

an ichor-thimble, before your fable's
over. *Caramba!* I hear you mumble
in the bell-bottom of some lush victrola,
shyly rehearsing a subtler number.

I Taught Myself

I taught myself to play the fiddle once,
bowing right at the bridge to starve the tone,
with chalk for rosin, making puffs of white
noise on the downbeat—

noise like the dust that finally silted up
the ancient parlor radio, way in the attic,
keeping its intestine ranks of tubes
dry as the drought years.

I taught myself to sing by breathing that dust
deep in my lungs, where it crackles now like static:
sweet to the sad girls, the trick of singing like
long ago sounds now.

Appendix

Just to the right—now, slightly further down—
the shy, unminded littlest daughter hangs.
With nothing much to do there on her own

she sleeps late, counts her many blessings, sings
old sailors' songs she surely wasn't taught
and dreams she'll marry a doctor. How she longs

to see herself discovered by his fleet,
mirroring scalpel! In the dark she swoons
with love, turns ripe, too ripe, implacably sweet.

Exile

For some years now I've lived in Exile:
long enough to pass for native
if there were any natives here,
which there are not.

The sand in Exile falls like rain.
It fills my glass,
the kind of sand that stands for time,
the kind of *like* that means *instead*.

Each of us says his evening prayers
to the star above a different town.
We couple, yes,
but always it's with someone else

and long ago.
I like you, though. I like you well,
the kind of well you drink from once
was cool and unforgettable.

Blazon

Wrist of mine, what do you have
to sing for yourself?
There where the light-shy lifeblood tests
the surface, like a curious fish.

Or shoulder? Hurdy-gurdy crank,
sing in your turn:
Do you remember throwing the stone?
Do you remember shrugging it off?

Collar bone, bent like a lyre,
or a coat hanger:
you're in on the shrug as well, I see.
Sing *everything depends, depends*.

A question to the chest returns
the hollow sound
of the heart repeating itself again,
as though that were an explanation.

(We skirt the belt, by tradition,
only recording
a steady, atavistic pulse
like the old-fashioned busy signal.)

Down to the knees, then: musical hinges,
a serenade!
Alas, it seems you've got the knack
of genuflecting noiselessly.

So it's up to the head: O head of mine,
this is your song.
It's the head calls the tunes, after all,
though you can hurt me anywhere.

Dichten = Condensare

Basil Bunting, fumbling about with a German-Italian dictionary, found that this idea of poetry as concentration is almost as old as the German language. 'Dichten' is the German verb corresponding to the noun 'Dichtung' meaning poetry, and the lexicographer had rendered it by the Italian verb meaning to condense.

(Ezra Pound, *ABC of Reading*)

The garbage men are talking trash,
deep in thought beside their truck:
the job provokes reflection on
essences and accidentals.

Paper or plastic? Glass or can?
Such distinctions seem to help.
There is naming at the end,
as there was in the beginning.

Meanwhile, things keep piling up:
strollers, hollow-boned, like birds;
the slender stem of a halogen lamp,
heliotrope, straight as a saint.

Someone wants to forget this stuff—
forget all about it—so the truck
clenches its brow, closes its mind
hard on the facts as it receives them.

Each thing makes its own wild cry.
Who thought, so many kinds of throat.
Under pressure all confess
I never knew what I was for.

Someone Left the Bed Ajar

Someone left the bed ajar:
the bedclothes billow in the storm
like curtains in a tall window;
rain-soaked sheets tangle and snap.

Who is out in a storm like this?
Besides the two of us, I mean.
Careless, not to make it fast,
the bed; and is the oven on?

Now the sheets have taken off:
they're flapping madly against the ceiling
and the bed stands altogether open.
The wind rushes through with unseemly haste.

Suppose you looked inside: you'd see
a deep recess of tangled trees,
like a dark road in a French movie,
trees tossed by the same wind,

tossed and turned and tangled together,
while just beyond the vanishing point
someone or other is setting out,
looking for a place to sleep.

It's Raining

It's raining. It's cold. It's dark. It's late.
What's raining? What's cold? What's dark? What's so late?
The clouds? Or the air? The sky? The day?
No. No. No, no.

Symmetry

Every tree has two shadows:
one that reels around the trunk,
one that's sunk in the dirt below.

Unlucky you, with only one
that follows you everywhere you leave,
the gray train of your wending sheet.

—Unless you have a double, too,
who stands down into the undergrowth
with his feet flat against your feet.

Imagine, everywhere you go
he has to work the earth beneath you,
face-first into that heavy weather,

the fossil storm of fallen leaves
that's always blowing underground.
Lunging he grabs for the roots like rungs.

If that were true, it would explain
too much. We should be glad to be
above the ground or under it.

Snow Apple

Frost-blight of an apple blossom starts a seed
deep in a snow-drift, somewhere far to the north,
by way, perhaps, of compensation: seed like a hailstone,
better, a pearl, elaborating apple-flesh
whiter than white around itself and crisp as—something—
tart as a—what—a bitter reminiscence of—

—do you remember? Yes, remember, yes, you do,
but in some part of your mind you've never gone before,
and not because you can't: it's just that it's cold up there,
cold, and far, and tracklessly white, and full of things
you can't fairly be said to have put there for yourself,
hanging there, as in the cold tree of the snowdrift.

It might be very interesting to go sometime.
But then, there are so many places you've always meant to get back to,
and when did you last go someplace you've never been before?
The snow apple ripens, and then it rots, disintegrating
into crystal. Down south, another apple blossom?
It's hard to know, although it does occur to you.

Acknowledgments

The author would like to thank the editors of the following journals and magazines where these poems first appeared, sometimes in different form:

Hopkins Review: "How Do You Do"; "Exile"

The New Yorker: "Rituals"

The Paris Review: "This is a City of Bridges"; "Splinter"; "Cantaloupe"; "Quarter"; "My Puppets"

Poetry London: "The Whale-Road"

Poetry Review: "Alcibiades's Waltz"

TLS: "Folding Star"; "Faith and Hope"; "The Labor Theory of Value"; "The Dressing Room"; "Dichten = Condensare"

Western Humanities Review: "Strawberries and Cream"

Yale Review: "Morning Czar and Evening Tsar"

Nick Barberio

Jeff Dolven grew up in Massachusetts and studied at Yale and Oxford. His poems have appeared in *The New Yorker, The Paris Review, The Times Literary Supplement, The Yale Review,* and elsewhere. *Speculative Music* is his first collection. He teaches poetry and poetics, especially of the English Renaissance, at Princeton University, and is an editor at large at *Cabinet* magazine. He lives in Brooklyn.

Sarabande Books thanks you for the purchase of this book; we do hope you enjoy it! Founded in 1994 as an independent, nonprofit, literary press, Sarabande publishes poetry, short fiction, and literary nonfiction—genres increasingly neglected by commercial publishers. We are committed to producing beautiful, lasting editions that honor exceptional writing, and to keeping those books in print. If you're interested in further reading, take a moment to browse our website, www.sarabandebooks.org. There you'll find information about other titles; opportunities to contribute to the Sarabande mission; and an abundance of supporting materials including audio, video, a lively blog, and our Sarabande in Education program.